English G 21

Das Ferienheft

A holiday trip with Tom and Jessica

B2

für Realschulen

Cornelsen

English G 21 • Band B 2 • Das Ferienheft
A holiday trip with Tom and Jessica

Herausgeber
Prof. Hellmut Schwarz, Mannheim

Erarbeitet von
Jennifer Seidl, M.A., München

In Zusammenarbeit mit dem Verlagsbereich Englisch
Dr. Christiane Kallenbach (Projektleitung);
Solveig Heinrich (verantwortliche Redakteurin)

Illustrationen
72dx4L, Berlin (S. 3)
Roland Beier, Berlin (wenn nicht anders angegeben)
Carlos Borrell, Berlin (S. 31: Stadtplan)
Sheila Seyfert-Menzel, Berlin (S. 48, hintere Umschlagseite: LernCoachies)

Titelbild
Roland Beier, Berlin (Illustrationen); IFA-Bilderteam, Ottobrunn (Hintergrund: Union Jack: Jon Arnold Images)

Umschlaggestaltung
Klein & Halm Grafikdesign, Berlin

Gesamtgestaltung und technische Umsetzung
graphitecture book, Rosenheim

Tonaufnahmen zu den Web-Codes
Sprecher – Laura Cameron, Martha Crowe, Nathan Crowe, Julian Dudley, Steve Ellery, Mala Ghedia, Marianne Graffam, Alexander Hale, Jesse Inman, Arabella Mathias, Reuben Potts, Katie Sherrard, Darren Smith
Studio – Clarity Studio Berlin
Tontechnik, Regie und Aufnahmeleitung – Christian Schmitz

www.cornelsen.de
www.EnglishG.de

1. Auflage, 1. Druck 2012

Druck: Himmer AG, Augsburg

ISBN 978-3-06-032924-3

Inhalt gedruckt auf säurefreiem Papier aus nachhaltiger Forstwirtschaft.

Liebe Schülerin, lieber Schüler,

wieder ist ein Schuljahr geschafft. Jetzt sind erst mal Ferien – Zeit zum Durchschnaufen!

Dass du trotzdem dieses Heft aufgeschlagen hast, ist toll. Vielleicht hast du einfach Spaß an Englisch oder du musst ein bisschen was wiederholen, damit im nächsten Schuljahr alles gut läuft. Auf jeden Fall haben wir das Ferienheft so gestaltet, dass es dir hoffentlich auch Spaß macht und das Lernen eher nebenbei passiert. Wenn es dich ein bisschen an ein Rätselheft erinnert, ist das genau richtig. Das Heft erzählt die Feriengeschichte von Tom und Jessica – aber nicht einfach zum Lesen. Du musst Rätsel lösen, ein bisschen kombinieren, Dinge finden, wenn du am Ende die Auflösung wissen willst.

Vor jeder Überschrift siehst du einen farbigen Punkt. Die Farbe sagt dir, zu welchem Bereich die jeweilige Übung gehört. In diesem Heft findest du:

- **24 Übungen zur Grammatik**
- **19 Übungen zum Wortschatz**
- **11 Übungen zum Hören**
- **11 Übungen zum Lesen**
- **5 Übungen zur Aussprache**

Die Hörtexte kannst du dir auf der Website www.cornelsen.de herunterladen. Rechts oben auf der Website klickst du auf „Web-Code". Darunter trägst du den zur Übung zugehörigen Web-Code ein.
Ein Beispiel: Bei Übung **6 Our holidays** gibst du den Web-Code: EG21-FH2-02 ein. Wenn du alle Hörtexte auf einmal herunterladen möchtest, so ist dies durch Eingabe des Web-Code: EG21-FH2-01 möglich. Die Nummer des Tracks steht neben dem Kopfhörersymbol in der Überschrift. Um die Hörtexte nachzulesen, gibst du den Web-Code: EG21-FH2-18 ein.

Der Lösungsteil beginnt auf Seite 50. Allerdings solltest du nicht gleich nach hinten blättern, wenn du nicht weiter weißt. Manchmal musst du ein bisschen knobeln.

Auf Seite 48 ist ein Quiz abgedruckt. Trägst du das aus zwei Teilen bestehende Lösungswort richtig auf www.lerncoachies.de ein, kannst du die LernCoachies in der Zeit vom 1. August bis 1. Oktober kostenlos testen. Weitere Informationen erhältst du auf der hinteren Umschlagseite. LernCoachies.de Besser lernen. Besser werden.

Have a good time with T&J!

Deine Englischredaktion

1 It's so boring

'Hurry up, Tom. The film starts soon and it's a long walk to the cinema,' said Jessica to her twelve-year-old brother.

'I'm just looking for my MP3 player. I can't find it anywhere. Maybe Jamie has taken it again,' said Tom.

'Jamie is only five. He doesn't take your stuff. That isn't fair, Tom. And you don't need your MP3 player at the cinema anyway,' answered Jessica.

'OK. OK. Hey, look, I've found it. It was under the comics. So come on, let's go, Jess.'

'Don't call me Jess! You know I don't like it. My name is Jessica,' she said loudly. 'Now, where's my purse? This is the second film this week, but I really want to see it.'

'Me too. I've already spent most of my pocket money. We've watched five DVDs, we've been to the new ice-cream place three times this week, we've been to the museum, and we've been to the swimming pool every day,' Tom added.

'I know. The weather is nice and warm, but the holidays are boring,' answered Jessica.

'All my friends have gone somewhere. Ben has gone to an international summer camp in France with his sister. Luke has gone to visit his cousins in Wales, and Ali has gone to New York with his family. They won a holiday there,' said Tom.

'Really? Cool! My friends have gone away too. Lucy is in Scotland on a horse-riding holiday and Chloe is in Spain,' added Jessica.

'Yes. Our friends are having a great time. They're all doing exciting things – and what about us? What are we doing? Nothing!

Why aren't we going to Italy like last year?

We had a great time there. We made a lot of friends. The food and the weather were fantastic.

The holidays are so boring at home. Nothing is happening,' said Tom.

'You know that mum and dad haven't got time for a holiday this year. And they had to buy a new car in spring, so maybe we haven't got enough money for a holiday. But we've still got another four weeks before school starts again, so let's wait and see. Maybe something exciting will happen.'

Read the text. Are the sentences right or wrong? Mark a letter.

		right	wrong
1	Tom is twelve years old.	M	S
2	Tom can't find his comics.	A	I
3	Jamie is younger than Tom and Jessica.	T	X
4	Tom and Jessica are going to the cinema again.	C	W
5	Tom has still got a lot of pocket money.	E	H
6	They haven't been to the swimming pool.	L	E
7	Jessica's friend Lucy has gone to Spain.	R	L
8	Jessica and Tom think holidays at home are boring.	L	K

If your answers are right, the letters tell you Tom and Jessica's family name. What is it?

Their name is ______________________.

2 Colour the pieces

Find and colour two parts of eight irregular verbs. Use a different colour for each verb. Then write a list.

infinitive	simple past
eat	ate

3 A postcard from Spain

Choose the correct verbs.

bought	played	took✓
danced	said	walked
hurt	saw	was
met	swam	went

Hi Jessica!

Here we are in Malaga! It's sunny all day. Yesterday morning we (1) a bus into town. It (2) hot but we (3) for hours – till our feet (4)! We (5) lots of old buildings, beautiful churches and a museum, but my brother (6) it was boring. For lunch we (7) some delicious strawberries from a street market. In the afternoon we (8) to the beach. We (9) in the sea and (10) ball games on the sand. Our hotel has lots of fun activities for kids, like a disco. I (11) a nice boy there! He (12) with me four times! His name is Matthew. ♥

Hope you're enjoying the holidays! See you soon.

Love, Chloe

Jessica Mitchell
15 Park Road
Coventry
CV2 3TL
England

1 took ______ 4 ______ 7 ______ 10 ______

2 ______ 5 ______ 8 ______ 11 ______

3 ______ 6 ______ 9 ______ 12 ______

4 What did Chloe write?

Read Chloe's postcard to Jessica in exercise 3 again. Then find the correct answers.

1 Did Chloe Wilson and her family go to Spain?
2 Was it hot and sunny?
3 Did they have lunch at a restaurant?
4 Were the old buildings interesting?
5 Did Chloe's brother like the museum?
6 Was it boring for kids at the hotel?
7 Did Chloe meet a nice boy at the kids' disco?

Yes, it was.
No, it wasn't.
Yes, they did. ✓
No, they didn't.
Yes, she did.
Yes, they were.
No, he didn't.

5 What's the weather like?

Match the sentences and pictures.

A It's windy.
B It's rainy.
C It's stormy.
D It's foggy.
E It's hot.
F There's snow on the mountains.
G It's cloudy.
H It's sunny.

1

2

3

4

5

6

7

8

1 *E* 2 ___ 3 ___ 4 ___ 5 ___ 6 ___ 7 ___ 8 ___

6 Our holidays 2 Web-Code: EG21-FH2-02

Listen to the friends Lucy, Ben, Chloe, Luke and Ali. They are talking about their holidays. Who's speaking? Write their names.

Lucy
Scotland

Ben
France

Chloe
Spain

Luke
Wales

Ali
New York

Speaker 1 is *Ben*. Speaker 2 is ______________. Speaker 3 is ______________.

Speaker 4 is ______________. Speaker 5 is ______________.

7 Countries puzzle

Where are the cities? Write the names of the countries. Then find the word down.

1 B R I S T O L
2 C A R D I F F
3 P A R I S
4 C O P E N H A G E N
5 B A R C E L O N A
6 G L A S G O W
7 R O M E

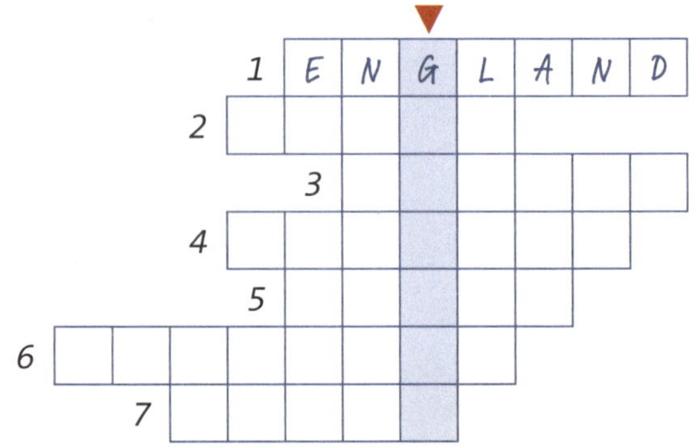

The correct answers give you the name of another country. Tom and Jessica would like to go there next year.

The country is: ______________________________.

8 Holiday activities 3 Web-Code: EG21-FH2-03

Listen to the five friends. What do they like best? Match the names with the holiday activities.

exploring new places
swimming in the sea
visiting castles and museums
making new friends
doing lots of sports

9 What do you hear? 4 Web-Code: EG21-FH2-04

Listen and write the correct sound in brackets [ ]. Does the word end with the sound [g] or [k]? Listen again and check.

1 [k] 2 [g] 3 [__] 4 [__] 5 [__] 6 [__]

7 [__] 8 [__] 9 [__] 10 [__] 11 [__] 12 [__]

10 Puzzle

Find words in the orange snake and write them down in the correct order. Then find the correct opposite in the green snake and complete the list in the puzzle.

1 poor – rich
2 ____
3 ____
4 ____
5 ____
6 ____
7 ____
8 ____

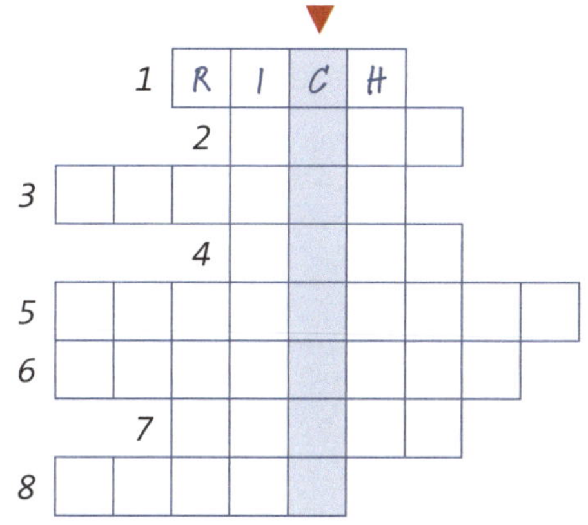

If your answers are right, the word down tells you where the Mitchells live.

The name of the city is C ____.

11 What's it about?

Look quickly at the text in exercise 12. What do you think it's about? Tick (✓) a box.

A ☐ the children's friends	C ☐ an invitation to Bristol
B ☐ last year's holiday	D ☐ healthy food

12 At dinner

Read the five text parts and put them in the right order. Write numbers 1 to 5 in the boxes.

☐ 'It was Megan,' said Mrs Mitchell when she came in from the kitchen with a big bowl of fruit salad. 'They've moved into their new house in Bristol and she's invited us all to go and visit them there for a week.'

'Oh, that's great. Aunt Megan and Uncle Dan are really nice. We always have fun with them. Uncle Dan always tells us funny stories. When can we go, Mum?' asked Tom.

1 At six thirty the Mitchells were having dinner.

'Can I have some more potatoes, please, Mum?' asked Jamie, still hungry[1].

'Of course you can, Jamie. Here you are,' said his mother.

'More potatoes for me too, please,' added Tom.

'And what about some more carrots?' asked their dad. 'You know they're good for you.'

'Erm, ...,' said Tom.

Before Tom could say 'no' the phone rang in the hall.

☐ 'But we'd really like to go. Right, Jess? This year the holidays are so boring,' said Tom.

'Yes, we'd like to go somewhere. And we've never been to Bristol. But wait ... I know, why can't Tom and I go alone? You needn't even drive us there. We can go by train. We're old enough,' said Jessica with a big smile.

'Oh, I didn't think of that,' answered their dad. 'Well, let's ask mum. Let's hear what she has to say about the idea ...'

☐ 'I'll go,' said Mrs Mitchell.

'The phone call can't be for us,' said Tom. 'All our friends have gone on holiday. I wonder who it is. Maybe we've won a holiday to New York too! That's the phone call to tell us!'

'I don't think so,' laughed Jessica.

[1] hungry ['hʌŋgri] *hungrig*

☐ 'Well, I'm afraid we can't go,' said their dad. 'You know that we haven't got much time at the moment. I have to work in the holidays this year,' said their father.

'And I have to stay at home to look after grandma. You know she's been ill and I go to see her every day. So I'm afraid we can't go to Bristol this summer,' Mrs Mitchell added as she left the room.

13 About Jessica and Tom

Complete the sentences with the right form of ***do*** *or* ***make****.*

1 Tom likes to write stories. He makes models of ships and planes too.

2 Jessica and Tom both ________________ sport. They like hockey and basketball.

3 Jessica likes school. She usually ________________ her homework before dinner.

4 Tom likes Maths best. He's good, but he sometimes ________________ mistakes.

5 Before the holidays he ________________ an interesting project for Geography.

6 Yesterday afternoon Jessica ________________ a chocolate cake for her dad's birthday.

7 Tom wanted to help, but Mrs Mitchell says that he always ________________ a mess in the kitchen.

8 Last week Tom helped his dad to paint the garage. They ________________ a good job.

14 Let's call Aunt Megan 5 Web-Code: EG21-FH2-05

Listen. Which statements are right? Mark the letter.

1	Tom calls Aunt Megan.	B
2	Tom likes to write detective stories.	R
3	Tom's favourite sport is tennis.	C
4	Jamie will go to Bristol too.	A
5	There's a famous bridge in Bristol.	U
6	Bristol has a zoo[1] too.	N
7	The Balloon Fiesta[2] starts on Wednesday.	B
8	Tom likes scary things.	E
9	The children will go to Bristol next Thursday.	O
10	Megan will meet the children at the station.	L

If your answers are right, the letters make a famous name in Bristol.

The name is ______________________.

[1] zoo [zu:] *Zoo, Tierpark* [2]Balloon Fiesta [bə'lu:n fiˌestə] *Heißluftballonparade*

15 What did they do in Bristol?

Complete the questions and short answers. Use the simple past.

Tom: Mum and dad have been to Bristol. Let's ask them what they did there.

Jessica: Good idea. Mum, when you were in Bristol, *(1)* did you drive (*drive*) over the Clifton Suspension Bridge?

Mum: Yes, *(2)* we did. It's amazing. It's more than 400 metres long.

Jessica: And *(3)* ______________________ (*look*) round the SS Great Britain?

Dad: No, *(4)* ______________________. There wasn't enough time. But you will have enough time to see it.

Tom: And *(5)* ______________________ (*go*) to the science centre?

Mum: Yes, *(6)* ______________________. You must go there too. It's really interesting. You'll love it.

Tom: And what about the pirate pubs? *(7)* ______________________ (*see*) any?

Mum: Of course. Yes, *(8)* ______________________. We had a drink in the Llandoger Trow. It's in King Street, near the harbour[1].

Jessica: And *(9)* ______________________ (*take*) a boat trip round the harbour?

Dad: No, *(10)* ______________________. It started to rain, so we went to St Nicholas Market.

[1]harbour ['hɑ:bə] *Hafen*

16 Travel words

Read the sentences. Then write travel words in the puzzle.

1 When it's raining, Jessica and Tom go to school by ...
2 Sometimes their mother takes them in the ...
3 When the weather is good, they go to school by ...
4 Last year the Mitchells went to Italy by ...
5 The children would like to fly in a ...
6 They want to take a ... trip round Bristol Harbour.
7 They would like to explore Brunel's ..., the SS Great Britain, too.

1	B	U	S							
2										
3	B									
4					E					
5							P			
6										
7										

Put the letters in the blue boxes in the right order to complete the sentence.

Jessica and Tom will go to Bristol by ______________________.

17 Clothes for Bristol

Label the pictures.

jeans ✓ pyjamas shorts socks sunglasses
tops trainers trousers T-shirts

1 
jeans

2 
______

3 
______

4 
______

5 
______

6 
______

7 
______

8 
______

9 
______

18 Let's get things ready

Underline the correct green words.

1 **Tom:** Where **is** / **are** my blue shorts, Mum?

2 **Mum:** I've washed **it** / **them**. **They were** / **It was** dirty.

3 **Jessica:** I need **some** / **a** new sunglasses. **This isn't** / **These aren't** very nice.

4 **Tom:** But you bought **a new** / **a new pair of** sunglasses last week. And I need **a** / **some** new trainers. I want some red and silver ones. They look so cool.

5 **Mum:** Are you going to take **those** / **that** new trousers, Tom? **It's** / **They're** in your wardrobe.

6 **Tom:** No, I don't think so. I'll take **two pairs of** / **two** jeans.

7 **Jessica:** Mum, **this isn't** / **these aren't** my new pyjamas. Where **is it** / **are they**?

19 Train tickets

Complete the dialogue with words from the box.

chat	copy	find out	install	send e-mails	surf✓

Jessica: We need train tickets for Wednesday. Maybe we can buy them online. It's often cheaper. But we must ask mum and dad first, because they have to pay.

Tom: Do you know how to do it? You know more about computers than me.

Jessica: Of course, but you can do it too. You can *(1)* surf the internet. You can *(2)* ______________ programmes. You can *(3)* ______________ with your friends. You can download music and pictures. You can *(4)* ______________ things for me, you can *(5)* ______________ to your e-friends. So you can *(6)* ______________ information about train tickets too. Try 'raileasy.co.uk'. It's a good website.

Five minutes later

Tom: OK. I've done it. Listen. We leave at 10.27 on Wednesday and arrive in Bristol at 12.41. We have to change trains once at Birmingham New Street. It's quite cheap for kids. Two tickets cost £ 36,50 – that's there and back. OK?

Jessica: Yes! Brilliant! Let's tell mum and dad what we've found out.

20 It's mine

Complete the dialogue with **mine, yours, hers, his, ours** *or* **theirs.**

Tom: Is this book *(1)* yours?

Jessica: Yes, it's *(2)* ________________. I'm going to read it on the train.

Tom: And what about this new blue exercise book? Whose is it?

Jessica: I don't know. I've asked mum. She says it isn't *(3)* ________________. So I thought it was maybe *(4)* ________________, Tom, for your stories.

Tom: No, it isn't. It must be dad's.

Jessica: No, I don't think it's *(5)* ________________. He uses his phone for notes.

Tom: OK, if nobody wants it, now it's *(6)* ________________. And Jessica, what about the new camera for Bristol?

Jessica: Well, the camera isn't *(7)* ________________, it's mum and dad's.

Tom: I know it's *(8)* ________________, but I think it would be great to take lots of photos of our holiday. I'm going to ask them tonight at dinner.

Jessica: Good idea. Good luck!

21 Whose things are they?

Write sentences.

The black sunglasses are Jessica's. | The exercise book is Tom's.

22 A visit 6 Web-Code: EG21-FH2-06

What's right? Choose and mark A, B or C.

1 Jessica and Tom visit ...
A a neighbour
B their grandmother
C an aunt

2 They take ... flowers[1].
A red and blue
B blue and yellow
C red and yellow

3 Grandma is ill. She has ...
A a stomach ache
B a cold and a headache
C a toothache

4 The train ride from Coventry to Bristol is ... long.
A two hours
B more than two and a half hours
C about two and a half hours

5 Jessica and Tom want to visit ... first.
A the Explore-at-Bristol science centre
B the Balloon Festival
C Brunel's ship

6 Tomorrow morning their train leaves at about ...
A half past nine
B half past ten
C half past eleven

[1] flower ['flaʊə] *Blume*

23 What do you hear? 7 Web-Code: EG21-FH2-07

Listen and mark the word that you hear. Does it end with the sound [d] or [t]? Listen again and check.

1 played – plate
2 sad – sat
3 hard – heart
4 heard – hurt
5 feed – feet
6 spend – spent
7 made – mate
8 build – built
9 hid – hit
10 had – hat
11 need – neat
12 lived – lift

Add the numbers of the words that end with the sound [t].
Is your answer '32'? That's correct!

24 At the station

Lots of people are waiting for trains. What are they doing? Complete the sentences. Use the present progressive of these verbs.

buy ✓ call chat eat get off push run say

1 A man *is buying* a newspaper.

2 A young man ________________ a bike.

3 Two women ________________.

4 An old man ________________ the train.

5 Two boys ________________ hamburgers.

6 A girl ________________ somebody on her mobile.

7 A man and his wife ________________ goodbye.

8 A little girl and her mum ________________ to the train.

25 Get it right!

Mark the group word. Look at the number in brackets ( ) and write the letter of the word.

1 cloudy	storm	windy	weather	sunny	weather	(5)	h
2 plane	travel	helicopter	train	boat	__________	(6)	____
3 food	tomatoes	lettuce	fish	cheese	__________	(4)	____
4 strawberry	orange	banana	fruit	apple	__________	(4)	____
5 granddaughter	aunt	family	uncle	granny	__________	(2)	____
6 install	computer	download	software	surf	__________	(2)	____
7 trousers	pyjamas	clothes	jacket	T-shirt	__________	(7)	____
8 throat	knee	heart	stomach	body	__________	(4)	____

Put the letters in the right order to find a word for something that everybody likes.

The word is h________________.

26 Remember!

At the station Jessica and Tom's parents tell them what they **must, mustn't** *or* **needn't** *do in Bristol. Complete the sentences with the right word.*

Dad: Look after the camera. You *(1)* mustn't lose it.

Mum: You *(2)* ________________ help Megan and Dan in the kitchen.

Mum: You *(3)* ________________ make your beds and keep your rooms tidy.

Dad: You *(4)* ________________ go to bed late.

Mum: You *(5)* ________________ mail us. We'll send e-mails.

Mum: If you go out alone, you *(6)* ________________ tell Megan where you're going.

Dad: You *(7)* ________________ lose your money or your mobiles. Be careful.

Mum: You *(8)* ________________ call home every day. We'll call you.

Dad: You *(9)* ________________ remember to send grandma a postcard.

Jessica: You *(10)* ________________ worry about us. We'll be fine.

27 What's the same?

Some verbs and nouns[1] have the same form. How many can you find? Mark them and write a list.

build call✓ describe explain glue invite
joke live love name plan rain
rehearse report ride smile teach visit walk

call, ______________________________

____

____

How many words have the same form? The correct answer tells you how old Tom is.

The answer is: ______________.

[1] noun [naʊn] *Substantiv, Nomen*

28 What do you hear? 8 Web-Code: EG21-FH2-08

Listen and say the words. Do they end with the sound [b] or [p]? Tick (✓) the right box.

	[b]	[p]
1		✓
2	✓	
3		
4		
5		

	[b]	[p]
6		
7		
8		
9		
10		

Tick (✓) the correct sentence.
- Four of the ten words end with the sound [b].
- Five of the ten words end with the sound [b].
- Six of the ten words end with the sound [b].

29 Find pairs

Find and write pairs of opposites.

COOL FOREGROUND

CLOSED

RIGHT beginning slow

open end top needn't

WARM fast BACKGROUND

MUST bottom left

cool – warm

30 On the train (1) 9 Web-Code: EG21-FH2-09

Listen to the text. Are the sentences right or wrong? Tick (✓) the correct box.

		right	wrong
1	The train to Bristol leaves at twelve minutes past eleven.	✓	
2	There aren't many people on the train.		
3	A man is wearing a blue jacket.		
4	The man jumps on the train just before it leaves the station.		
5	The man is sitting on the left side of the train.		
6	The second man is smaller than the first man.		
7	The first man drops something and the second man picks it up.		

31 From the train window (1) 10 Web-Code: EG21-FH2-10

What do Jessica and Tom see from the train window? Listen and write the correct numbers.

32 From the train window (2)

Now write the words for the numbers in 31.

1 hill	6	11
2	7	12
3	8	13
4	9	14
5	10	15

33 On the train (2)

Jessica: Tom, stop watching those men. It's rude. They're probably just friends. Not everybody is a spy, you know.
Tom: It's OK. They can't see me. They're too far away. But maybe you're right. I don't really think they're spies. The second man has gone anyway.
Jessica: Hey. The train is going slower now. Are we stopping?
Tom: No, I don't think so. We aren't near a station. We're in the middle of a field. I'm taking photos of cows and sheep. We don't see many farm animals in Coventry. Click. Click. Hey, we really *are* stopping. I wonder why. Hey, look, Jess! Somebody has jumped off the train! It's a man in a dark jacket. I saw him through the camera. Look, that's him. He's running towards the village – with a big bag.

Jessica: Yes, I can see him. Maybe he lives there and he's in a big hurry to get home. But you can't just jump off a train – not without a good reason. Quick, Tom. Take a photo!
Tom: OK! That was quite exciting. Hmm. I'm hungry now. I know! I'll go and buy some sandwiches.
Jessica: Sandwiches? Well, at least *that*'s a good idea.
Tom: Erm ... Do you want ham[1], cheese and tomato – or cheese, tomato and ham?
Jessica: Ha, ha, Tom! Here is some money from dad. And a bottle of water for me, please.
Tom: OK. Oh, the train is going fast again now. I won't be long.
Jessica: You needn't hurry. My book is exciting!

Ten minutes later
Tom: Jess, here you are. Sandwiches and water. But listen, something important. Our man on the train in the black jacket – he's gone! I can't see him anywhere.
Jessica: You mean, you think ... *he* jumped off the train? Maybe you were right about him.

[1] ham [hæm] *Schinken*

Read the text. Tick (✓) the correct statements and cross (✗) the wrong statements.

1	Tom is sure that the two men are spies.	✗
2	The train suddenly goes slower.	
3	Tom sees that a man has jumped off the train.	
4	Jessica's book is boring.	
5	Tom buys some sandwiches and a bottle of lemonade for Jessica.	
6	Tom thinks the man in the black jacket has jumped off the train.	

34 What's what?

Find and colour three parts of eight irregular verbs. Use a different colour for each verb. Then write a list in the order: infinitive, simple past, past participle.

take

ate

drunk

gave

been

eaten

see

thrown

went

drink

taken

was/were

saw

gone

given

throw

threw

be

go

eat

give

seen

drank

took

be – was/were – been

35 What they have done

Complete the sentences with the present perfect. Then match the sentences with letters A–E.

1 Jessica and Tom have taken (*take*) the train to Bristol. [C]

2 Jessica ________________ (*take*) an exciting book with her. [ ]

3 Tom ________________ (*eat*) his sandwiches. [ ]

4 The children ________________ (*call*) Aunt Megan. [ ]

5 The man in the black jacket ______________________________ (*disappear*). [ ]

A She's reading it now.

B So he isn't hungry now.

C They're sitting in the train now. ✓

D Tom can't see him anywhere.

E She's going to meet them at the station soon.

36 Find the words

Find eight more words and write them with their opposites.

B	U	Y	L	S	K
E	P	L	O	V	E
F	O	W	S	W	P
O	S	G	E	R	U
R	S	A	T	O	T
E	I	O	E	N	*
W	B	D	R	G	O
I	L	L	K	M	N
B	E	N	E	M	Y
T	E	A	C	H	P

▶	▼
buy – sell	before – after
________________	________________
________________	________________
________________	________________
________________	________________

37 Welcome to Bristol!

'Hello, you two! Welcome to Bristol and welcome to 43 Clifton Road! Did you have a good trip?' asked Dan with a big smile. 'Megan says this is your first time here.'

'That's right, Uncle Dan. Aunt Megan says there's lots to see and do in Bristol,' said Jessica.

'Yes, there is. You'll like it here. There's a holiday programme for kids too, visits, activities, sports and lots of other things. And the neighbours' kids are waiting to meet you. I'm sure they'll show you things and tell you all about the kids' programme. You'll all have lots of fun. Has Megan shown you your rooms? Have you taken your bags upstairs? And has she given you a tour of the house?'

'Yes, we've taken our stuff upstairs. And our rooms are really nice. But we haven't had a tour of the house yet. It's bigger than our house,' Tom answered. 'You've got a nice garden too.'

'Yes, you can see our special visitor later – a hedgehog. He comes to visit us every evening. He walks round the garden and then he disappears under the big tree in the corner. We call him Charlie. Have you ever had a hedgehog?'

'No, we haven't. We've never had a pet,' said Jessica, 'but maybe we will one day.'

'Well, erm … I don't have to work today, so I've just made lunch. I've cooked lasagne with salad. I hope you're hungry. After lunch the neighbours' kids are coming to say hello. They've got a friend from Germany at their house too. Can you speak German?' asked Uncle Dan.

'No, we can't,' answered Tom.

Just then Megan came into the kitchen.

'Listen, all of you. I've just heard on the radio that a man robbed a bank near Birmingham New Street station this morning. So the police think he probably got a train to London or maybe even to Bristol. They think that maybe the man had a partner too. He stole over twenty-five thousand pounds.'

'Really? Oh dear. Do the police know what the man looks like? Has anybody given the police a description?' asked Dan.

Jessica and Tom said nothing. They just listened with eyes wide open …

Read the text. Write short answers.

1 Is there lots to see and do for kids in Bristol? Yes, there is.

2 Have Jessica and Tom met the neighbours' kids yet? ______________________

3 Have the children taken their bags upstairs? ______________________

4 Does Charlie visit Dan and Megan in the evenings? ______________________

5 Does Dan have to work today? ______________________

6 Has Megan made lunch? ______________________

7 Are they going to have lasagne for lunch? ______________________

8 Can Jessica and Tom speak German? ______________________

9 Did Megan hear about the bank robber on TV? ______________________

10 Did the bank robber steal more than £25,000? ______________________

38 Welcome to Clifton Road

Cross out (X) the wrong sentences. Circle the numbers after the correct sentences.

1	a	Jessica and Tom have already arrived in Clifton Road.	10
	b	~~Jessica and Tom have arrived already in Clifton Road.~~	7
2	a	They haven't yet had a tour of the house.	2
	b	They haven't had a tour of the house yet.	5
3	a	Jessica and Tom have never had a pet.	9
	b	Jessica and Tom never have had a pet.	11
4	a	Uncle Dan already has cooked lasagne for lunch.	8
	b	Uncle Dan has already cooked lasagne for lunch.	13
5	a	Aunt Megan just has heard about a bank robber on the radio.	14
	b	Aunt Megan has just heard about a bank robber on the radio.	6

Add the numbers after the correct sentences.
The correct answer tells you Megan and Dan's house number in Clifton Road.

The house number is: ______________

39 Find the animals

Megan and Dan have a hedgehog in their garden. Circle the names of more animals in the word square. Then label the pictures.

hedgehog

H	E	D	G	E	H	O	G	H	E
W	O	O	D	P	E	C	K	E	R
R	F	A	V	F	R	O	G	O	U
R	F	O	X	I	T	E	A	N	I
M	M	O	L	E	A	L	S	A	R
D	E	E	R	E	S	Q	U	I	R
R	E	R	A	B	B	I	T	L	S

Write a sentence with the other letters. Which animals does Jessica like best?

____

40 What will they do?

*Complete with **'ll (will)** or **won't**.*

Tom: We *(1)* 'll have to go to the police and tell them what we saw.

Jessica: Are you sure? Maybe they *(2)* _______________ think we're mad.

Tom: No, they *(3)* _______________. They *(4)* _______________ want to know lots of details.

Jessica: What about Aunt Megan and Uncle Dan? *(5)* ________________ you tell them what you saw?

Tom: I don't think so. Not now. Later. Maybe they *(6)* ________________ think our information is very important anyway. Let's go to the police station. I'm sure they *(7)* ________________ listen to us there.

41 Hi!

Read all the sentence parts first. Then match them.

The neighbours' kids, Amita and Ranjit, have a visitor from Germany. Her name is Lena. They have all come to meet Jessica and Tom. They are talking about where they'll go and what they'll do if ...

Ranjit: If you like old ships,	1	A	if it rains.
Amita: We'll go shopping at St Nicholas Market	2	B	we'll do the free tour of the Georgian House.
Amita: We'll go to the At-Bristol centre	3	C	we'll take you to a pirate pub.
Ranjit: If you want to see the Clifton Suspension Bridge,	4	D	we'll show you the SS Great Britain.
Ranjit: If you want to know what Brunel looked like,	5	E	we'll show you his statue near the station.
Amita: If you like big old houses,	6	F	if you speak more slowly.
Ranjit: If you like pirate stories,	7	G	we'll walk over it and take photos.
Lena: I'll understand you better	8	H	if you like science.

1 D 2 ___ 3 ___ 4 ___ 5 ___ 6 ___ 7 ___ 8 ___

42 Jessica's holiday diary (1)

Read Jessica's diary for the first day of their trip to Bristol. Complete the text with verbs in the simple past.

Wednesday August 8

Today (1) was (be) quite exciting! At Birmingham New Street a man in a black jacket (2) got (get) on the train, just before it (3) __________ (leave) the station. The man (4) __________ (make) a lot of phone calls on his mobile. Then another man (5) __________ (join) him. They (6) __________ (be) both nervous. Tom likes to play detective, so he (7) __________ (think) the men were thieves or spies. The train (8) __________ (go) quite slowly for a few minutes. Suddenly a man (9) __________ (jump) off the train! He (10) __________ (look) like the man in the black jacket. We (11) __________ (~~be~~) sure, but we (12) __________ (~~see~~) him again on the train.

Later Aunt Megan (13) __________ (hear) something on the radio about a bank robber. The police think that maybe he (14) __________ (get) on a train to Bristol! Was it our train? Was it the man in the black jacket? Was the second man his partner? We (15) __________ (~~tell~~) Aunt Megan and Uncle Dan about it. We'll tell them later. Tom thinks we have to go to the police. I think he's right.

We (16) __________ (meet) the neighbours' kids. They're OK. I'm sure they'll help us. I think this is going to be an interesting holiday ...

43 Finding the way 11 Web-Code: EG21-FH2-11

Jessica and Tom ask the way to the police station. They are in Elizabeth Street. Which person tells them the right way? Person A, B or C? Follow the map.

Person ________ tells Jessica and Tom the right way.

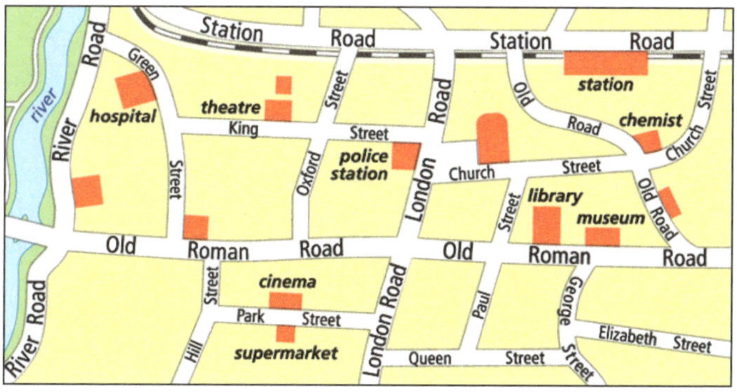

44 What are we going to say?

Write correct sentences.

Jessica: What /at the police station / going to / are / we / say

1 What are we going to say at the police station?

Jessica: you / going to / the photos / show / Are

2 ______________________________?

Tom: They won't want to see sheep and cows! We / going to / about the men / 're / tell the police

3 ______________________________.

Jessica: you / What / tell them / going to / are

4 ______________________________?

Tom: Everything. How the first man jumped on the train, the phone calls, his black clothes, the big bag.

But / 'm not / going to / I / the second man / describe

5 ______________________________.

He was smaller. I'm sure about that – says Tom Mitchell, famous detective!

45 At the police station (1)

'Come on, let's go in. Don't be nervous,' said Jessica as she pushed Tom through the main door of the police station.

'I'm not nervous – well, maybe just a bit,' answered Tom. 'I've never been inside a police station before.There are so many people here. Who are we going to talk to?' asked Tom as he looked round.

Suddenly a voice behind them said, 'Hello, you two. What can we do for you? Another stolen bike?'

'Oh, hello. No, we don't want to report a stolen bike. We have some information – about the Birmingham bank robber. We think we saw him – and his partner,' said Jessica.

'Oh really? Well, let's start with your names,' said the policeman in a friendly voice. He sat down at his desk.

'We're Tom and Jess – erm … we're Thomas and Jessica Mitchell, from Coventry,' said Tom.

'From Coventry. I see. Now, why do you think you saw the Birmingham bank robber, and why do you think he had a partner?' the policeman wanted to know.

Tom and Jessica told the policeman about the man with a big bag who jumped on the train to Bristol at the last minute, about the phone calls and the second man. Then they told him that somebody jumped off the train – and he was wearing a dark jacket and he had a big bag – just like the first man. The policeman listened. Then he said, 'I think Detective Fox would like to hear your story. It's his case. I'll try to find him. Just wait here. Don't go away.' He disappeared through a glass door.

'You see, Jess, he listened. He thinks our story is true. I'm going to tell Detective Fox all the details. Tell him what you saw too. We'll tell him everything. This is all so exciting. We'll be really important – you'll see,' said Tom with a big smile.

After five minutes the policeman came back. Two men were with him. Tom looked at the men.

'But … I don't understand …,' he said suddenly. 'Look, Jess! It's the two men from the train … What are they doing here …?'

'This is Detective Fox and his assistant Detective Simpson …' the policeman said.

Tom was puzzled. Detectives? Did the policeman say the men were detectives? Was all this just a bad dream?

Read all the sentence parts first. Then match them. Put in **because, when, so** *or* **but**.

Tom was a bit nervous	1	A	______ Tom was happy.
The children didn't know who to talk to	2	B	______ there were so many policemen.
The policeman thought the story was interesting,	3	C	______ he saw the two men with the policeman.
Tom was very puzzled	4	D	______ they were detectives.
The children thought the men were bank robbers	5	E	when they went into the police station.

1 E 2 ___ 3 ___ 4 ___ 5 ___

46 Plans

Amita, Ranjit and Lena are talking about what they are going to do. Complete the dialogue with words from the boxes.

're going to ✓ | Are you going to | are we going to | 's going to | are going to | 'm not going to | aren't going to

Amita: Tomorrow we *(1)* 're going to take you to the Balloon Fiesta, Lena. You'll love it. We can ask Jessica and Tom. Maybe they'll go too. Ranjit has got a new camera. He *(2)* ______ take lots of photos. Right, Ranjit? Mum and dad *(3)* ______ see the festival this year because they haven't got time.

Lena: And what *(4)* ______ do today?

Amita: Well, it's sunny, and it's the holidays. I *(5)* ______ stay at home. What about a picnic?

Ranjit: OK. Great idea! Let's have a picnic in the park. *(6)* ______ make the sandwiches, Amita?

Amita: Yes, I am. And you and Lena *(7)* ______ help me!

47 It's more exciting

*Compare. Write sentences with the correct form of the word in brackets ( ) and **than**.*

Ranjit: What are we going to do at the weekend? Maybe the Explore-at-Bristol? I think it's *(1)* more interesting than (*interesting*) the Georgian House.

Amita: Yes, I agree. And the SS Great Britain is *(2)* ____________________ (*good*) the British Empire and Commonwealth Museum.

Ranjit: I think Tom, Jessica and Lena will like the Balloon Fiesta. It's *(3)* ____________________ (*famous*) other balloon festivals in England.

Amita: Let's go to St Nicholas Market after the Balloon Festival or to a famous pirate pub.

Ranjit: OK, but I think a smoothie from the Big Banana juice bar is *(4)* ____________________ (*healthy*) cola at a pub.

Amita: You're right, but I think smoothies are *(5)* ____________________ (*expensive*) cola.

Ranjit: Then there's the zoo. The monkeys are great.

Amita: Or what about shopping? I'm sure Lena would like to see our department stores. Maybe they aren't *(6)* ____________________ (*big*) German stores but I'm sure they're different.

Ranjit: Oh, no. Not shopping again. Nothing is *(7)* ____________________ (*bad*) department stores!

48 At the police station (2) 12 Web-Code: EG21-FH2-12

Listen and mark the right answers.

		right	wrong
1	Detective Fox was on the 11.12 train to Bristol.	H	M
2	The village was about twenty minutes away from Bristol.	A	L
3	The man was wearing a red baseball cap.	L	O
4	Tom would like some red and gold trainers for this birthday.	E	S
5	The man had an earring in his right ear.	E	R
6	Tom is proud because they helped the police.	M	P

In the correct order the letters give you the name of another very famous detective.

The name is Sherlock H_______________.

49 Are you a good detective? 13 Web-Code: EG21-FH2-13

Listen to the text in exercise 48 again. Do you think the bank robber looks like A, B or C?

I think the bank robber looks like ________.

Why do you think so? Write two sentences.

I think so because he's got ______________________________

______________________________.

He's wearing ______________________________.

50 Jobs

Look for eleven more jobs. Circle them.

D	E	T	E	C	T	I	V	E	A
U	E	N	G	I	N	E	E	R	N
T	C	A	R	E	T	A	K	E	R
M	E	P	A	I	N	T	E	R	G
D	O	C	T	O	R	A	N	I	S
P	R	E	S	E	N	T	E	R	A
B	U	S	*	D	R	I	V	E	R
T	E	E	X	P	L	O	R	E	R
A	F	I	R	E	M	A	N	C	H
P	A	R	A	M	E	D	I	C	E
W	R	I	T	E	R	R	S	P	Y

Write a sentence with the other words. What is Aunt Megan's job?

____

51 What do you hear? 14 Web-Code: EG21-FH2-14

Say the words in the box and match them to the correct CD. Then listen and check.

bear chair cheer deer first hear heard hurt their we're where word

bear		

52 Group words

Find the group words and write them at the top of the correct list. Then complete the five lists with the other words.

Transport				
train	actor	factory	week	sea

53 Jessica's holiday diary (2)

Complete with the correct form of the word in brackets ( ).

Thursday — August 9

Today was so exciting! Tom and I went to the police station! We told Detective Fox and his assistant about the man who jumped from the train. Tom didn't see him very (1) clearly (clear) because he was running (2) _______________ (fast), but Detective Fox listened (3) _______________ (careful). I told him about the church with the bell[1] tower in the village where the man jumped out. He made notes, and he said they would find it (4) _______________ (easy). Tom's photo was great. We looked at it in detail on the computer, and we saw an earring in the man's right ear! Detective Fox said we did (5) _______________ (good).
Tom left the police station really (6) _______________ (happy). 'My photo was very important', he said (7) _______________ (proud).
Now the police are going to work (8) _______________ (hard) to find the man.
In the afternoon we went to an ice-cream place with Ranjit, Amita and Lena, the girl from Germany. We told them about our visit to the police station. We all laughed (9) _______________ (loud) about Tom's mistake – he thought the two detectives were bank robbers! Lena didn't understand everything, so we told her the story again, (10) _______________ (slow). Now Tom looks at people on the streets – he's looking for a man with an earring and red and silver trainers. He really likes playing detective. Probably we'll go to Bath with the neighbours' kids next week.
Mum and dad called to chat. We didn't tell them about Tom's mistake or about our visit to the police station. They'll worry too much!

[1] bell [bel] *Glocke*

54 He must be somewhere

Complete the sentences with a word from the box.

anybody anything anywhere everything everywhere✓ nobody
nothing somebody something✓ somewhere

Tom: There must be *(1)* something that we can do to help to catch the bank robber. Let's look in the shops, in the cafés and on the streets.

Ranjit: Well, we're trying hard. When we're in town we look *(2)* everywhere for a man with an earring. I saw four or five this morning.

Amita: But we haven't seen *(3)* ____________ with an earring and red and silver trainers.

Jessica: But the thief must be *(4)* ____________. There was *(5)* ____________ on the radio about him. I asked Aunt Megan, but she hasn't heard *(6)* ____________.

Lena: But I think the police don't tell *(7)* ____________ they know.

Tom: That's right, Lena. Maybe they found *(8)* ____________ in the village who fits the description. Maybe they've already caught him.

Jessica: I don't think so. He can be in Bristol, in London or *(9)* ____________ now. Maybe he's hiding, or maybe he thinks he's safe because *(10)* ____________ saw him.

Tom: Well, I saw him. But I hope he doesn't know that. I think I'll wear my sunglasses.

55 Which parts go together?

Find and match two words that make a new word.

head pocket sun juice web
phone cycle police door bank

glasses money path station ache
site call robber bell bar

One word: sunglasses, ____________

Two words: police station, ____________

____

56 Find the word

Complete with the correct word.

1 Tom and Jessica left Coventry on Wednesday.	at (H) / on (I)
2 ________ the train Tom bought some sandwiches and water.	On (S) / In (U)
3 Tom took a photo ________ the man who jumped out of the train.	from (N) / of (P)
4 Aunt Megan met the children ________ the station.	at (N) / by (T)
5 Aunt Megan heard about the bank robbers ________ the radio.	in (E) / on (M)
6 Jessica and Tom gave the police important information ________ the man.	about (S) / over (B)
7 Now the police are looking ________ the bank robber.	after (Y) / for (O)

Put the letters after your answers in the correct order. They give you the name of Detective Fox's assistant.

His name is Detective ____________________.

57 Silent letters 15 Web-Code: EG21-FH2-15

Say the words. Find and circle the silent letters. How many more words can you find? Listen and check your answers.

listen answer wolf hour castle Roman Wednesday

would climb knee lists sandwich planet half glue

Mark the correct number.

There are 6 8 10 more words with silent letters.

58 Zoo and farm animals

Jessica would like to go to Bristol Zoo. Which animals can you see in zoos? Which are farm animals? Look at the pictures. Write the names of the animals in two groups.

ZOO ANIMALS		FARM ANIMALS	
elephant	______	duck	goat
______	______	______	______
______	______	______	______
______	______	______	

59 Jessica's holiday diary (3)

Read the four text parts and put them in the right order. Write numbers 1 to 4 in the boxes.

☐ We walked back to the town centre and looked at our photos of the Fiesta. Lena's new shoes hurt her, so we walked slowly. Lena tries to speak English all the time. She sometimes makes mistakes, but we understand her and we sometimes laugh – and she laughs too.
She told us about her school in Germany and about her family. She's got two super pets – a cat called Ruben and a parrot called Rocky. He sometimes says bad things – like Tom! In town we bought some ice creams. I had banana, Ranjit had kiwi and lemon, Amita had vanilla and chocolate. Tom dropped his strawberry ice cream on his trainers. Now he really needs new ones!

☐ At home we had a barbecue in the garden. The neighbours came too. Uncle Dan's steaks were a bit too well done ☹ – but Mrs Patel brought some great Indian food and saved the party. ☺ We all played football in the garden after that. It was great fun. The girls won! ☺
Mum called and we told her about the Balloon Fiesta and the barbecue – not about the bank robber. It's getting dark now, so it will be time to see Charlie – the hedgehog – soon.

☐ Ranjit wanted to take us to the Balloon Festival, so we got a bus at Rupert Street. It was so exciting.
There were hundreds of fantastic balloons in the blue sky! People come with their balloons from lots of different countries. We met some people from Germany, so Lena was happy. There are so many other things to see and do too – shows, live concerts with cool bands, lots to eat and drink at the food market, so we had a snack for lunch. We took lots and lots of photos.

[1] Today was really great. After breakfast we helped Aunt Megan in the kitchen and then we tidied our rooms. At 10 we met Ranjit, Amita and Lena in the shopping centre just a short bus ride away.
First we looked round the music shops. Ranjit bought a CD and later he bought some comics. I bought a postcard for gran. We had a drink in a café and I wrote the card. All the time we were looking for a man with an earring. I wonder if we'll ever see him – I don't think I want to be face to face with a bank robber!

60 What's correct?

Read exercise 59 again and mark the correct answer.

1 At ten o'clock Jessica and Tom ...

[S] helped in the kitchen [C] met the neighbours' kids [R] went shopping

2 Who bought something at the shopping centre?

U Ranjit and Amita	C Ranjit and Tom	H Ranjit and Jessica

3 The children ... to the Balloon Fiesta.

S walked	A took a bus	B cycled

4 They had lunch ...

O at home	E at a café in the shopping centre	R at the Balloon Fiesta

5 They walked back to town slowly because ...

L Lena's feet hurt	C it was so hot	K they were tired

6 Rocky is a ...

N cat	P hedgehog	I parrot

7 What kind of ice cream did Tom have?

O chocolate and vanilla	E strawberry	R kiwi and lemon

Now write the letters after your answers. If they are correct, you have written the name of Megan and Dan's night visitor.

The name is ______________________.

61 Correcting mistakes

Lena sometimes makes mistakes. There's one mistake in each sentence. Mark and correct five more mistakes.

1 I always have had a pet. My favourite pet is Rocky. I have always had a pet.

2 Tomorrow I show you photos of Rocky and my family. ______________________

3 I am always going to school by bike. ______________________

4 My brother goes not to the same school. ______________________

5 My brother is better at English as me. ______________________

6 I'm sure the police find the bank robber soon. ______________________

62 Places in town

Jessica, Tom and their friends saw these places and shops in town. Write the words in the puzzle and find the word down.

1 You can get a train here.
2 When you're ill you sometimes have to go here or stay here.
3 This is where you can report a bank robber!
4 You can buy tickets to see a play or a musical here.
5 Here you can buy food and drinks and lots of other small things.
6 You can buy things for a cold, a temperature or a headache here.
7 You can buy stamps and send letters from here.
8 You can buy everything here, from clothes to things for your home.

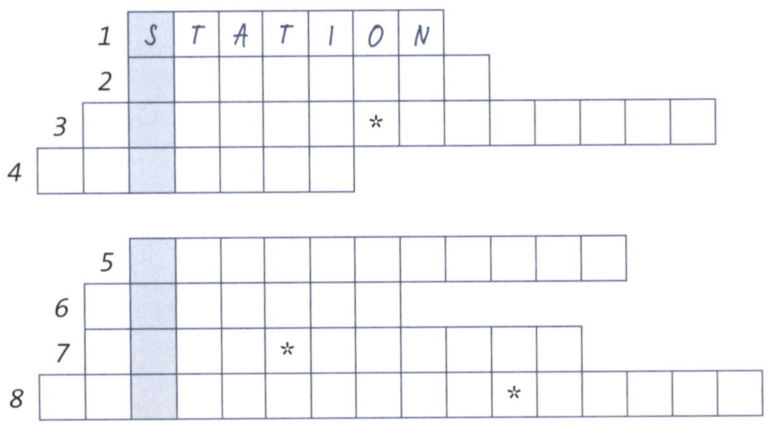

If your word down is correct, it tells you where Tom would like to go to choose his birthday present.

The answer is S____________________.

63 Shops in our area

Amita tells Jessica and Tom about shops in the area. Read the text and label the shops.

'The bus stops in front of the department store. When you go into the shopping centre, you see a chemist on the right.
There's a café between the chemist and the sports shop. They have very good ice cream there.
Next to the sports shop there's a shoe shop. The last shop is a big supermarket.
On the other side, next to the supermarket and opposite the shoe shop there's a good pizza restaurant. We go there sometimes. Between the pizza restaurant and the music shop there's a bike shop.
Behind the chemist and the café there's a bank, and the post office is next to it. There's a very

good Indian restaurant at the end of the street, next to a book shop. We go there quite often. Oh, and the bus stops in front of the book shop too.'

64 Let's go to Bath!

Choose what is correct. Cross out the wrong words.

1 The children want to go ~~tomorrow~~ to Bath tomorrow.
2 They have to be at the bus station at 9.53 at the bus station.
3 They'll arrive at 10.41 in Bath at 10.41.
4 They needn't be before 11 o'clock at the Herschel Museum before 11 o'clock. That's when it opens.
5 They want to go to the Roman Baths before lunch to the Roman Baths.
6 They can go after lunch to Bath Abbey after lunch. It's near the Baths.
7 The girls want to go to the Fashion Museum in the afternoon to the Fashion Museum.
8 They have to be back in Bristol at six o'clock back in Bristol.

65 In a café in Bath

'I really enjoyed today. Bath is a great place. I loved the Herschel Museum,' said Tom with a big smile.

'I think we learned a lot about William and his sister Caroline. Uranus is the seventh planet from the Sun and the third largest of the nine planets. Is that right, Jessica? Anyway, it was all very interesting. Just imagine how exciting it was to discover a planet!'

'Yes, and Caroline was the first woman astonomer,' added Lena.

'And we loved the Fashion Museum,' said Amita. It was so cool, and I think we learned a lot too. The Roman Baths were OK, but not as exciting as the museums.'

'Well, who's thirsty?' asked Ranjit.

'I am,' answered Jessica.

'Me too,' said Lena.

'OK. Then let's go for a drink,' said Tom. 'I'm sure we'll find a café somewhere near here. We can look at all our photos then. Or we can look for men with earrings and cool trainers.'

'You're still playing detective, Tom, but I think we have to leave it to the police now. They'll find him. Ranjit, do you know where there's a café or an ice-cream place?' asked Jessica.

'No, I don't, but we'll find one near the Abbey, I'm sure. Look, over the road down there. People are sitting outside, so it must be a café. Come on. Let's go.'

…

'Well, it's quite full, but with a bit of luck we'll get a table,' said Amita. 'What about over there? Look, I think those people are just leaving.'

'It's nice here. The ice creams look really big!' said Amita.

'Ice cream makes me thirsty. I'm going to have some lemonade – a very big glass' said Ranjit.

'I'm going to have my favourite ice …' Suddenly Tom stopped in the middle of his sentence.

'Hey, Tom,' began Ranjit. 'What's the matter? Are you OK?' At first Tom didn't speak and he didn't move. After some seconds he said quietly, 'Who's got a piece of paper and something to write with? Now, please. Quickly …!'

Read the text. Are the sentences right or wrong? Mark the correct letters.

		right	wrong
1	William Herschel's sister was called Catherine.	C	W
2	Uranus is the third largest planet.	A	H
3	Uranus is the sixth planet from the Sun.	E	T
4	The children visited the Fashion Museum too.	B	T
5	They enjoyed the Roman Baths more than the museums.	O	S
6	They are hungry after their tour of the city.	C	R
7	They look for a café close to the Abbey.	R	L
8	They have to wait to get a table.	A	E
9	Ranjit is going to have a glass of lemonade.	Y	O
10	Tom is going to have ice cream.	R	E

Put the letters after your answers in the correct order. If your answers are correct, the letters tell you which ice cream is Tom's favourite.

Tom likes ______________________ ice cream best.

66 What did Tom write?

Find the code and write the message.

2 7 20 '18   14 7 7 5   3 7 9 20 2!   18 22 12   19 6 20 5

D O N 'T

3 7 19 19 12 3   11 13   13 11 18 18 11 20 23   19 12 22 11 20 2

10 7 9!   11   6 1   13 9 3 12!   22 12   22 6 13

6   13 20 6 5 12   18 6 18 18 7 7   7 20   22 11 13

3 11 23 22 18   6 3 1.   11   3 12 1 12 1 19 12 3

18 22 6 18   20 7 16.   8 12 13 13,   15 6 14 14

2 12 18 12 15 18 11 4 12   17 7 21!

67 Jessica's call 🎧 16 Web-Code: EG21-FH2-16

Round the corner from the café Jessica calls Detective Fox. Listen to the call. Tick (✓) the correct statements and cross (✗) the wrong statements.

1 ☑ Detective Fox remembers Tom and Jessica.
2 ☐ The police don't know where the bank robber is.
3 ☐ The man in the café has a tattoo on his arm and leg.
4 ☐ Tom remembers now that the man on the train had a snake tattoo.
5 ☐ Jessica isn't scared.
6 ☐ Detective Fox is in Bristol.
7 ☐ Detective Fox will call the police in Bath.
8 ☐ He will tell them to send two men in uniform.

68 Bristol and Bath quiz

What do you know about Bristol and Bath? Do the quiz. Mark the right letter.

1 St Nicholas is the name of a … in Bristol.	I church	T train station	J market
2 The Llandoger Trow is a …	P museum	A juice bar	I pirate pub
3 The Clifton Suspension Bridge is over … long.	M 400 m	B 500 m	S 600 m
4 The Bristol Balloon Fiesta takes place in …	E July	B August	A September
5 Brunel was a famous …	G writer	L explorer	I engineer
6 The SS Great Britain is a …	L science centre	G ship	P plane
7 Herschel was a famous …	G astronomer	R engineer	M writer
8 Herschel discovered the planet …	O Pluto	Y Venus	S Uranus

If your answers are correct, they give you the name of the bank robber.

His name is __ __ __   __ __ __ __ __.

69 What was everybody doing when ...?

Complete with the verbs in brackets in the past progressive.

When the detectives from Bath arrived at the café Tom *(1)* was sitting (*sit*) with his friends.

He *(2)* ______________________ (*wear*) his sunglasses and *(3)* ______________________ (*watch*) the bank robber. Ranjit *(4)* ______________________ (*drink*) lemonade and Amita *(5)* ______________________ (*eat*) a big chocolate ice cream. Lena *(6)* ______________________ (*write*) a text on her mobile. The four friends were very quiet. They *(7)* ______________________ (*chat*). Tom *(8)* ______________________ (*tell*) jokes. The friends *(9)* ______________________ (*wait*) nervously. What was going to happen?

Jessica *(10)* ______________________ (*hide*) behind the corner of the café. She *(11)* ______________________ (*talk*) to Detective Fox on her mobile.

The bank robber *(12)* ______________________ (*call*) the waiter[1]. Was he going to pay and leave the café?

[1] waiter ['weɪtə] *Kellner*

70 Surprise[1], surprise! 17 Web-Code: EG21-FH2-17

Now listen to the end of the story.

[1] surprise [sə'praɪz] *Überraschung*

Die Transkripte zu den **Hörtexten** können bei Eingabe des Web-Codes EG21-FH2-18 heruntergeladen werden.

1 It's so boring

	1	2	3	4	5	6	7	8
right	M		T	C				L
wrong		I			H	E	L	

Their name is **Mitchell**.

2 Colour the pieces

infinitive	simple past
eat	ate
buy	bought
do	did
fly	flew

infinitive	simple past
make	made
meet	met
see	saw
swim	swam

3 A postcard from Spain

1 took
2 was
3 walked
4 hurt
5 saw
6 said
7 bought
8 went
9 swam
10 played
11 met
12 danced

4 What did Chloe write?

1 Yes, they did.
2 Yes, it was.
3 No, they didn't.
4 Yes, they were.
5 No, he didn't.
6 No, it wasn't.
7 Yes, she did.

5 What's the weather like?

1 E *2* H *3* B *4* G
5 D *6* A *7* C *8* F

6 Our holidays 2 EG21-FH2-02

1 Ben *2* Luke *3* Lucy *4* Ali *5* Chloe

7 Countries puzzle

				1	E	N	G	L	A	N	D
			2	W	A	L	E	S			
					3	F	R	A	N	C	E
			4	D	E	N	M	A	R	K	
				5	S	P	A	I	N		
6	S	C	O	T	L	A	N	D			
		7	I	T	A	L	Y				

The country is: **Germany**.

8 Holiday activities 3 EG21-FH2-03

Lucy: making new friends
Ali: exploring new places
Chloe: swimming in the sea
Ben: doing lots of sports
Luke: visiting castles and museums

9 What do you hear? 4 EG21-FH2-04

1 [k] *5* [g] *9* [g]
2 [g] *6* [k] *10* [g]
3 [k] *7* [k] *11* [k]
4 [g] *8* [k] *12* [g]

10 Puzzle

1 poor – rich
2 win – lose
3 leave – arrive
4 strong – weak
5 cheap – expensive
6 boring – exciting
7 clean – dirty
8 sad – happy

		1	R	I	C	H			
			2	L	O	S	E		
3	A	R	R	I	V	E			
			4	W	E	A	K		
5	E	X	P	E	N	S	I	V	E
6	E	X	C	I	T	I	N	G	
		7	D	I	R	T	Y		
8	H	A	P	P	Y				

The name of the city is **Coventry**.

11 What's it about?
C

12 At dinner
3 – 1 – 5 – 2 – 4

13 About Jessica and Tom
1 makes
2 do
3 does
4 makes
5 did
6 made
7 makes
8 did

14 Let's call Aunt Megan 5 EG21-FH2-05
1 B *2* R *5* U *6* N *8* E *10* L
The name is **Brunel**.

15 What did they do in Bristol?
1 did you drive
2 we did
3 did you look
4 we didn't
5 did you go
6 we did
7 Did you see
8 we did
9 did you take
10 we didn't

16 Travel words

1	B	U	S							
2	C	A	R							
3	B	I	K	E						
4	P	L	A	N	E					
5	H	E	L	I	C	O	P	T	E	R
6	B	O	A	T						
7	S	H	I	P						

Jessica and Tom will go to Bristol by **train**.

17 Clothes for Bristol
1 jeans
2 trousers
3 trainers
4 pyjamas
5 sunglasses
6 shorts
7 tops
8 socks
9 T-shirts

18 Let's get things ready
1 is / <u>are</u>
2 it / <u>them</u>; <u>They were</u> / It was
3 <u>some</u> / a; This isn't / <u>These aren't</u>
4 a new / <u>a new pair of</u>; a / <u>some</u>
5 <u>those</u> / that; It's / <u>They're</u>
6 <u>two pairs of</u> / two
7 this isn't / <u>these aren't</u>; is it / <u>are they</u>

19 Train tickets
1 surf
2 install
3 chat
4 copy
5 send e-mails
6 find out

20 It's mine
1 yours
2 mine
3 hers
4 yours
5 his
6 mine
7 ours
8 theirs

21 Whose things are they?
The black sunglasses are Jessica's.
The book is Jessica's.
The shorts are Jessica's.
The mobile phone is Jessica's.
The MP3 player is Jessica's.

The exercise book is Tom's.
The bag is Tom's.
The red sunglasses are Tom's.
The jeans are Tom's.
The crisps are Tom's.

22 A visit 6 EG21-FH2-06
1 B *2* C *3* B *4* C *5* A *6* B

23 What do you hear? 7 EG21-FH2-07
1 plate
2 sad
3 hard
4 hurt
5 feed
6 spent
7 made
8 build
9 hid
10 hat
11 neat
12 lived

1 + 4 + 6 + 10 + 11 = 32

24 At the station

1 is buying
2 is pushing
3 are chatting
4 is getting off
5 are eating
6 is calling
7 are saying
8 are running

25 Get it right!

1 weather
2 travel
3 food
4 fruit
5 family
6 computer
7 clothes
8 body

The word is **holidays**.

26 Remember!

1 mustn't
2 must
3 must
4 mustn't
5 needn't
6 must
7 mustn't
8 needn't
9 must
10 needn't

27 What's the same?

call, glue, joke, love, name, plan, rain, report, ride, smile, visit, walk
The answer is: **12**

28 What do you hear? 8 EG21-FH2-08

	[b]	[p]
1		✓
2	✓	
3		✓
4	✓	
5		✓

	[b]	[p]
6	✓	
7		✓
8		✓
9	✓	
10	✓	

Five of the ten words end with the sound [b].

29 Find pairs

cool – warm
beginning – end
bottom – top
foreground – background
needn't – must
open – closed
right – left
slow – fast

30 On the train (1) 9 EG21-FH2-09

	1	2	3	4	5	6	7
right	✓			✓	✓	✓	✓
wrong		✓	✓				

31 From the train window (1) 10
EG21-FH2-10

32 From the train window (2)

1 hill
2 castle
3 valley
4 forest
5 bridge
6 river
7 field
8 lake
9 factory
10 village
11 farm
12 sheep
13 cows
14 traffic
15 railway

33 On the train (2)

1	2	3	4	5	6
✗	✓	✓	✗	✗	✓

34 What's what?

be – was/were – been
drink – drank – drunk
eat – ate – eaten
give – gave – given
go – went – gone
see – saw – seen
take – took – taken
throw – threw – thrown

35 What they have done

1 have taken C
2 has taken A
3 has eaten B
4 have called E
5 has disappeared D

36 Find the words

B	U	Y	L	S	K
E	P	L	O	V	E
F	O	W	S	W	P
O	S	G	E	R	U
R	S	A	T	O	T
E	I	O	E	N	*
W	B	D	R	G	O
I	L	L	K	M	N
B	E	N	E	M	Y
T	E	A	C	H	P

▶

buy – sell
love – hate
ill – well, healthy
enemy – friend
teach – learn

▼

before – after
possible – impossible
lose – find, win
wrong – right
put on – take off

37 Welcome to Bristol!

1 Yes, there is.
2 No, they haven't.
3 Yes, they have.
4 Yes, he does.
5 No, he doesn't.
6 No, she hasn't.
7 Yes, they are.
8 No, they can't.
9 No, she didn't.
10 Yes, he did.

38 Welcome to Clifton Road

1a	*1b*	*2a*	*2b*	*3a*	*3b*	*4a*	*4b*	*5a*	*5b*
10	X	X	*5*	*9*	X	X	*13*	X	*6*

The house number is: **43**

39 Find the animals

hedgehog

woodpecker

mole

fox

deer

rabbit

frog

H	E	D	G	E	H	O	G	H	E
W	O	O	D	P	E	C	K	E	R
R	F	A	V	F	R	O	G	O	U
R	F	O	X	I	T	E	A	N	I
M	M	O	L	E	A	L	S	A	R
D	E	E	R	E	S	Q	U	I	R
R	E	R	A	B	B	I	T	L	S

Her favourite animals are squirrels.

40 What will they do?

1 we'll/will
2 they'll/will
3 they won't
4 They'll/will
5 Will you
6 they won't
7 they'll/will

41 Hi!

1 D *2* A *3* H *4* G *5* E *6* B *7* C *8* F

42 Jessica's holiday diary (1)

1 was
2 got
3 left
4 made
5 joined
6 were
7 thought
8 went
9 jumped
10 looked
11 weren't
12 didn't see
13 heard
14 got
15 didn't tell
16 met

43 Finding the way 11 EG21-FH2-11

Person **C** tells Jessica and Tom the right way.

44 What are we going to say?

1 What are we going to say at the police station?
2 Are you going to show the photos?
3 We're going to tell the police about the men.
4 What are you going to tell them?
5 But I'm not going to describe the second man.

45 At the police station (1)

1 E – when *2* B – because *3* A – so
4 C – when *5* D – but

46 Plans

1 're going to
2 's going to
3 aren't going to
4 are we going to
5 'm not going to
6 Are you going to
7 are going to

47 It's more exciting

1 more interesting than
2 better than
3 more famous than
4 healthier than
5 more expensive than
6 bigger than
7 worse than

48 At the police station (2) 12 EG21-FH2-12

	1	2	3	4	5	6
right	H				E	M
wrong		L	O	S		

The name is Sherlock **Holmes**.

49 Are you a good detective? 13 EG21-FH2-13

I think the bank robber looks like **B**.
I think so because he's got **an earring in his right ear, dark hair, a dark baseball cap, a dark jacket and a big bag.**
He's wearing **red and silver trainers.**

50 Jobs

D	E	T	E	C	T	I	V	E	A
U	E	N	G	I	N	E	E	R	N
T	C	A	R	E	T	A	K	E	R
M	E	P	A	I	N	T	E	R	G
D	O	C	T	O	R	A	N	I	S
P	R	E	S	E	N	T	E	R	A
B	U	S	*	D	R	I	V	E	R
T	E	E	X	P	L	O	R	E	R
A	F	I	R	E	M	A	N	C	H
P	A	R	A	M	E	D	I	C	E
W	R	I	T	E	R	R	S	P	Y

Aunt Megan is a teacher.

51 What do you hear? 14 EG21-FH2-14

[eə] – hair: bear, chair, their, where
[ɪə] – here: cheer, deer, hear, we're
[ɜː] – her: first, heard, hurt, word

52 Group words

Transport: train, plane, ship, the underground
People: actor, caretaker, engineer, paramedic
Buildings: factory, castle, hospital, post office
Time: week, minute, month, year
Holidays: sea, beach, lake, swimming

53 Jessica's holiday diary (2)

1 clearly
2 fast
3 carefully
4 easily
5 well
6 happily
7 proudly
8 hard
9 loudly
10 slowly

54 He must be somewhere

1 something
2 everywhere
3 anybody
4 somewhere
5 nothing
6 anything
7 everything
8 somebody
9 anywhere
10 nobody

55 Which parts go together?

One word: sunglasses, doorbell, headache, website
Two words: police station, bank robber, cycle path, juice bar, phone call, pocket money

56 Find the word

1 on *2* On *3* of *4* at *5* on *6* about *7* for
His name is Detective **Simpson**.

57 Silent letters 15 EG21-FH2-15

with silent letters: listen, answer, hour, castle, Wednesday, would, climb, knee, sandwich, half, glue
There are **10** more words with silent letters.

58 Zoo and farm animals

Zoo animals: elephant, bear, camel, hippo, kangaroo, lion, monkey, rhino
Farm animals: duck, goat, chicken, cow, horse, rabbit, sheep

59 Jessica's holiday diary (3)

3 – 4 – 2 – 1

60 What's correct?

1 C *2* H *3* A *4* R *5* L *6* I *7* E
The name is **Charlie**.

61 Correcting mistakes

1 I always have had a pet.
correct: I **have always had** a pet.
2 Tomorrow I show you photos of Rocky and my family.
correct: Tomorrow **I will show** you photos ...
3 I am always going to school by bike.
correct: I **always go** to school by bike.
4 My brother goes not to the same school.
correct: My brother **doesn't go** to the same school.
5 My brother is better at English as me.
correct: My brother is better at English **than** me.
6 I'm sure the police find the bank robber soon.
correct: I'm sure the police **will** find the bank robber soon.

62 Places in town

1			S	T	A	T	I	O	N							
2			H	O	S	P	I	T	A	L						
3		P	O	L	I	C	E	*	S	T	A	T	I	O	N	
4	T	H	E	A	T	R	E									

5			S	U	P	E	R	M	A	R	K	E	T			
6		C	H	E	M	I	S	T								
7		P	O	S	T	*	O	F	F	I	C	E				
8	D	E	P	A	R	T	M	E	N	T	*	S	T	O	R	E

The answer is **shoe shop**.

63 Shops in our area

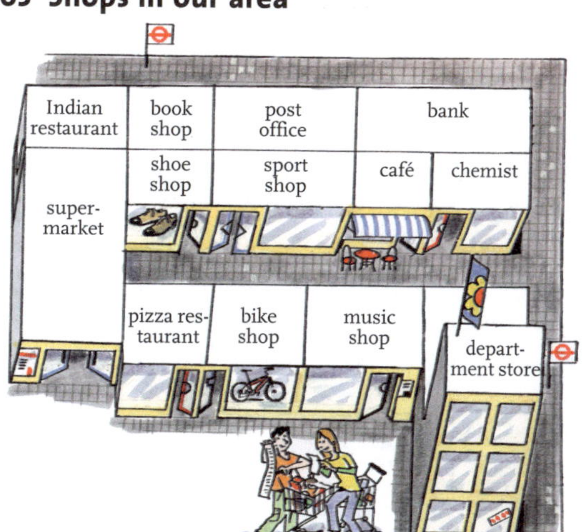

64 Let's go to Bath!

1 The children want to go ~~tomorrow~~ to Bath tomorrow.
2 They have to be at the bus station at 9.53 ~~at the bus station~~.
3 They'll arrive ~~at 10.41~~ in Bath at 10.41.
4 They needn't be ~~before 11 o'clock~~ at the Herschel Museum before 11 o'clock. That's when it opens.
5 They want to go to the Roman Baths before lunch ~~to the Roman Baths~~.
6 They can go ~~after lunch~~ to Bath Abbey after lunch. It's near the Baths.
7 The girls want to go to the Fashion Museum in the afternoon ~~to the Fashion Museum~~.
8 They have to be back in Bristol at six o'clock ~~back in Bristol~~.

65 In a café in Bath

	1	2	3	4	5	6	7	8	9	10
right		A		B			R		Y	R
wrong	W		T		S	R		E		

Tom likes **strawberry** ice cream best.

66 What did Tom write?

1	2	3	4	5	6	7	8	9	10	11	12
M	D	R	V	K	A	O	J	U	Y	I	E

13	14	15	16	17	18	19	20	21	22	23
S	L	C	W	F	T	B	N	X	H	G

Don't look round! The bank robber is sitting behind you! I am sure! He has a snake tattoo on his right arm. I remember that now. Jess, call Detective Fox!

67 Jessica's call 16 EG21-FH2-16

1	2	3	4	5	6	7	8
✓	✓	✗	✓	✗	✓	✓	✗

68 Bristol and Bath quiz

Mit dem Passwort erhältst du in der Zeit vom 1. August bis 1. Oktober Zugang zum Online-Lernportal zum Schulbuch, zu den LernCoachies. Siehe auch Informationen auf der Rückseite des Ferienheftes.

69 What was everybody doing when …?

1 was sitting
2 was wearing
3 was watching
4 was drinking
5 was eating
6 was writing
7 weren't chatting
8 wasn't telling
9 were waiting
10 was hiding
11 was talking
12 was calling